THE STORY OF THE MARION BOTTLING COMPANY

by

Wythe M. Hull, Jr.

Library of Congress Catalog Card Number: 85-073444

ISBN   0-89227-113-2

Commonwealth Press, Inc.
415 First St.
Radford, VA 24141

PRINTED IN THE UNITED STATES OF AMERICA

THE HISTORY
OF
MARION BOTTLING
COMPANY, INC.

by

Wythe M. Hull, Jr.

THIS BOOK IS DEDICATED TO:
MY FELLOW EMPLOYEES OF
MARION BOTTLING COMPANY, INC.
FROM 1929 TO 1983
WHOSE LOYALTY AND EFFORTS
MADE IT POSSIBLE

Chapter I

The story of Marion Bottling Company from the date of its birth as a corporate entity to the present time is what I shall attempt to relate, largely from memory, but in some considerable degree backed by facts from the files of the company. The story will be of the company from January 3, 1929 to the present. However, as a preface to the story in this locality, it is necessary to give a brief review of the history of soft drinks in Smyth County, Virginia.

As far as I have been able to find out the very first soft drinks to appear in Smyth County were made by Mr. J. L. Thornton, who started the business in either 1905 or 1907. As a boy I remember Mr. Thornton, whose store was located on Main Street about where Home & Auto Supply Company is now located. It was a frame building and an 'ell' on the building extended over to approximately where the Parks Belk Store is. It was in this part of the building that the manufacturing of soft drinks, or "pop" as it was known in my young days, took place.

As I recall it, and as I have heard others say, the soft drink firm had no delivery fleet of its own other than a wheelbarrow that Bertram Thornton, (son of J. L. Thornton), used to deliver the firm's products to the local merchants. A portion of the firm's business was done with out-of-town merchants who ordered by mail. The orders were packed in shipping cases and were delivered to the railroad freight station by Mr. H. B. Sprinkle's dray wagon. I can remember seeing this wagon being loaded with cases to be shipped. There were as many as six or eight cases shipped in a single day.

In those days there was quite a different procedure used in the manufacturing of soft drinks than is used today. W. S. (Mike) Johnson, who was an employee of Marion Bottling Company until his death in 1950, was an employee of Mr.

Marion Bottling Company's first Bottling Plant. Date: Approximately 1912. Man in center with cap: W. S. (Mike) Johnson. Mike worked for Marion Bottling Company all his life. He was the bottling company's oldest employee in years of service when he died in 1950.

Thornton in those early days and he described to me in detail some of the procedures they used.

The carbonated water used in the products was manufactured in the plant by dripping hydrochloric acid on marble chips and catching the gas from the reaction in a bell-shaped contraption. The gas was then induced into the water by putting water in a tank, connecting the gas supply by a hose, and agitating the water and gas in the tank by rocking the tank on a set of rockers similar to those used on a rocking chair.

In those days the syrup was made by Mr. Thornton and he was very secretative and mysterious about the formula he used. Mike Johnson said that as long as he worked for Mr. Thornton he would not allow him to see him mix the syrup, although in all other phases of the business he was allowed to take full responsibility. This prepared syrup was measured (or guessed at) into bottles which had previously been washed in a tub of soapy water. In order to cleanse the insides of the bottles, lead shot was put in the bottle with the soapy water and shaken vigorously. Then shot and water were emptied into the tub and the bottle was rinsed by holding it over a rinsing tube attached to the water supply.

The bottles were filled on a machine that had a table that had two bottle positions. In the first position the bottle received the carbonated water. The bottle was then moved by hand to the crowning position where a crown was applied by placing the crown by hand in the crowning head and then stepping on a foot pedal which applied pressure to crimp the crown on the bottle.

As one can well see, the daily production of such a plant was limited.

The first bottles used by Mr. Thornton's plant were known as Hutchinson stopper bottles. We now have on display in our plant at least two of these old bottles that were used between 1905 and about 1909 when the "New Process" crown was invented. The stopper bottle was so constructed that a wire in

3

the neck of the bottle held the stopper which was inside the bottle. After the bottle was filled with the carbonated drink the wire was pulled up by a hook so that the washer or stopper in the bottle was pulled up against the neck of the bottle thereby sealing the bottle. A shake of the bottle built up the pressure in the bottle so that it stayed sealed. When it came time to open the bottle, a blow delivered by hand on the loop of wire, pushed the stopper down into the bottle and the contents were ready for consumption. The loud noise resulting from this method of opening the bottle was where the name "pop" originated.

So much for the details of the preparation of the product in those early days. It is enough to say that the volume of the business was not great. We have no details as to what the annual sales were or what the selling price was. We do know that the retail price was five cents and that the bottle size was regularly a six ounce capacity.

Mr. Thornton continued to operate the bottling plant as an adjunct to this store from its beginning in 1905 or 1907 until his death in 1914. After his death the business was carried on by his widow and his son Bertram Thornton. World War I caused a sugar shortage and a labor shortage and we are told that operations at the bottling plant were suspended for approximately six months at one time. Sugar prices reached a wholesale level of thirty-five cents a pound and for a short time the wholesale price of soft drinks rose to $1.50 per case. However, with the decline of sugar to its traditional price of three and one-half cents to four cents per pound, the wholesale price of soft drinks dropped to seventy cents per case of 24.

In 1921, the bottling business was purchased from the Thornton family by a partnership of two veterans of World War I, B. Scott Sprinkle and N.E. Robinson. The location of the business was moved from the Main Street location to a portion of the old abandoned Marion & Rye Valley Railroad Depot on Railroad Avenue. The business was operated from that location until 1931, when it was moved to a new building on North Main Street.

1925 Orange Crush Bottling Co. Marion, Virginia.
Left to Right: B. Scott Sprinkle, N. E. Robinson, George Sprinkle, Paul Thompson, Mike Johnson, Unknown.

About 1921, (no exact date has been found) new competition appeared on the scene for the partnership of Sprinkle & Robinson in the bottling business. A new company came to town and set up shop in the Francis Building on the corner of North Main Street and Depot Street. It was named The 3 C Nectar Bottling Company and it bottled and sold a soft drink called 3 C Nectar. We are told that the name came from the parent company, Columbia Chemical Company of Roanoke, Virginia. The drink was a cola type drink and was widely advertised by the painted wall signs and barn roof signs. The two persons who came to Marion to operate the plant were later to become two of Marion's best known and respected citizens, Mr. Quincy Calhoun and Mr. F.A. Roland.

The company was organized as a corporation and one of their promotional gimmicks was to sell every merchant who handled soft drinks a share of stock in the company, thus encouraging them to push the product for better sales. It was said that stock certificate book was used very much as a check book and other items such as automobiles, etc. were purchased with stock certificates in the new company by its president, a Mr. Carmichael, of Roanoke.

Fortunately for Sprinkle and Robinson, the new competition did not last long. In about eighteen months, the parent company, The Columbia Chemical Company, went bankrupt and shut down. This put their bottling plants out of business as they only had the one drink to bottle. The local plants then went into bankruptcy and the idea of selling stock to every merchant as a sales tool had a reverse reaction, thus benefiting Sprinkle & Robinson with their older business.

This was the very short history of Smyth County's second bottling company.

Sprinkle and Robinson worked energetically for several years and expanded the business to a considerable extent. In 1922, they secured the franchise to bottle Orange Crush and its accompanying Lemon Crush, Lime Crush and Grape Crush.

From 1921 to 1929, the roads in this section of Virginia were being improved to the extent that truck deliveries were becoming possible in several directions. A hard surfaced road was completed to Bristol as well as eastward to Roanoke. This opened up possibilities that previously had not existed in the operation of the bottling business. It was in these years that business was solicited by Orange Crush Bottling Company in both Bristol and Pulaski.

In the year of 1927, a new bottle washer and bottle filling machine was installed in the Marion bottling plant. This bottle washer was a four-wide Meyer - single compartment machine and was considered to be the very best bottle washing machine available at that time. The bottle filling machine made by Crown Cork & Seal Co. of Baltimore was a Dixie machine. This machine had a capacity of 24 bottles per minute or a case a minute, which was considered to be a high production rate for a bottle filling machine. Many bottlers located in large population centers who needed more production than 24 bottles per minute simply ordered more units of this machinery combination as their needs warranted.

Shortly after the new machinery was installed in Marion, Mr. Sprinkle and Mr. Robinson decided to move the old machinery, which was an old Baltimore semi-automatic filler and a Miller Hydro washer, to Pulaski and to establish a branch plant there. This was done after securing the Orange Crush franchise in that area.

It was about this time that the two partners in the business began having serious dissension and arguments between themselves. As a consequence, sales suffered a considerable decline in the years 1927 and 1928. Records left behind showed a decline from about 30,000 cases in 1925 to about 12,000 cases in 1928. This, of course, brought profits down until they turned into losses for these last two years - 1927 and 1928. This was the situation we found when we purchased the assets of the partnership in December 1928.

7

Chapter II

On January 3, 1929, Marion Orange Crush Bottling Co., Incorporated became a corporate entity that has lasted from that time to the present. A change in name was made by amendment to the charter in 1942, which changed the corporate name to Marion Bottling Company, Incorporated. This corporation was the purchaser of the assets, liabilities and business of the partnership of Sprinkle and Robinson.

As stated previously the official birth date of the corporation was January 3, 1929. However, negotations for the purchase of the assets of the old partnership were begun during the Thanksgiving weekend of 1928. It was then that Mr. James R. Shanklin and the writer had the first discussions with the owners of the business. The relationship between Mr. Sprinkle and Mr. Robinson had deteriorated to the extent that they would not meet in the same room with each other. I well remember that we would first talk with Mr. Sprinkle in the little office of the bottling plant, and get a proposition from him to take out in the main bottling room, and discuss it with Mr. Robinson. This process went on for a considerable length of time until we were able to come to an agreement that all parties could subscribe to. Finally, a proposition was worked out whereby the assets and liabilities of the partnership in the Marion area would be sold to the new corporation for a cash payment of $1,774.00. This payment went to B. S. Sprinkle with the understanding that the corporation would assume the obligations of the partnership not to exceed the amount of $6,200.00. B.S. Sprinkle would also receive all assets of the old partnership located in Pulaski as settlement in full for his share of the business. N. E. Robinson would receive a 1/3 interest in the new corporation as well as being relieved of his share of the debts of the old partnership. James R. Shanklin and W. M. Hull, Jr. provided

$1,174.00 and $600.00 respectively to pay B. S. Sprinkle his cash settlement. The corporation later repaid $774.00 to James R. Shanklin.

This was the agreement that was finalized on January 19, 1929 and the corporation authorized by the State Corporation Commission on January 3, 1929 became a reality. At the first meeting of the shareholders on January 19th the following directors were elected:

> James R. Shanklin ...... 50 Shares
> W. M. Hull, Jr. .... 30 Shares
> N. E. Robinson .... 40 Shares

Officers were: James R. Shanklin-President, W. M. Hull, Jr.-Secretary-Treasurer

The opening balance sheet at that time showed the company had actual assets of $13,751.95 and had debts of $7,227.30 which left an equity for the stockholders of $6,524.65. It was from this very modest beginning that the present company has developed.

As shown in the foregoing, N. E. Robinson, one of the two partners who preceded the corporation became one of the stockholders and a director of the new corporation. It was agreed among the new stockholders that Mr. Robinson would remain as an employee of the company for so long as his services were needed, provided he remained sober and able to satisfactorily perform his duties. One of the causes of his disagreement with Mr. Sprinkle, his former partner, was his addiction to strong drink. Needless to say, it was only a matter of a few weeks until Mr. Robinson was unable to report for work. After several instances, some of which necessitated someone going out on the route and driving the truck home because of his condition, Mr. Robinson was discontinued as an employee.

After getting a number of advances of money against his shares of stock, a personal deal between Mr. Shanklin and Mr. Robinson resulted in Mr. Shanklin acquiring the shares of stock owned by Mr. Robinson. The transaction was finalized on January 13, 1931.

Chapter III

Now - returning to the story of the operation of the new corporation. In early 1929, it is recorded that the company had five employees at that time. There were Wythe M. Hull, Jr. - General Manager, W. S. Johnson - syrup mixer and bottler, N. E. Robinson, E. N. Legard, K. O. Helton - salesmen. In addition, Howard Petty was employed part time as a helper in the bottling room. Salaries were very modest with the General Manager being paid a salary of $150.00 per month. W. S. Johnson was paid $17.50 per week for six ten hour days, or more, if needed. N. E. Robinson, E. N. Legard and Kyle O. Helton were each paid $21.00 per week for six days of work.

The plant was located in an old frame building that at one time was used as the freight station for the Marion & Rye Valley Railroad. On the outside it was boarded up and down for the side walls. The bottling room ceiling and side walls were finished on the inside with wood. The floor was wooden with a concrete platform for the machinery to sit on. A small room about six feet by ten feet was partitioned off as an office. The bottling room was heated in the winter by a large pot-bellied coal stove, and the office had a small edition of the same.

All bottles and cases were carried by hand from the truck to the bottle washing machine and the filled bottles and cases were carried again to the trucks to be hauled to the trade. There was no case conveyor at all, but the company did own a small floor truck that was occasionally used in handling bottles and cases. In addition to the bottle washing machine, (a 4-wide Meyer Jr. washer), the bottle filling machine, (a Dixie Model A), a carbonater, (a Perfection) - the company also had a chocolate cooking retort (3 basket size). Thus, the company had a rated capacity of 24 bottles per minute if everything worked perfectly. It was rare that capacity was reached. Since sales rarely reached one hundred cases a day even in the hottest days of summer this was adequate production machinery for our needs.

Our delivery fleet consisted of two trucks that were operational - a 1927 Reo truck which became our #1 and a Graham-Dodge truck of about the same year model which we designated as truck #2. E. N. Legard was the driver of #1 and Kyle O. Helton was driver of #2. The company had acquired two more old Reo trucks as part of the original package, but as neither of them had engines that could be operated it was decided early that it would be wise to buy a new truck. Consequently, early in 1929 we purchased a 1929 model Chevrolet truck from the J. E. Thomas Chevrolet Company of Marion. It became our #3 truck.

Accurate records of the operation of the business prior to 1929 were never located, but from what records we were able to assemble, it was estimated that about 12,500 cases were sold during the entire year of 1928. Naturally it was evident that sales must be increased if the company was to be able to stay in business. A lot of study and guessing revealed that one of the most serious obstacles to increased sales was the lack of confidence that the merchants had in the company. Prior to the formation of the new corporation no schedule of service was maintained. It was only when the notion hit one of the partners that a route was worked. Consequently, the new company decided to develop and work regular routes on regular set days. Likewise, it was decided to always refund deposits on empty bottles when the dealer so requested. It was also decided to follow a course of quality control that insured good products be delivered on each and every delivery. These measures were adopted and even though we had some very discouraging results at first, our sales efforts eventually began to show some results. Sales by the end of the year had increased from about 12,500 cases in 1928 to about 34,490 cases in 1929. Thus our dollar volume was about $25,868 for 1929, and our profit and loss statement as of December 31, 1929 showed a profit of $432.97.

Chapter IV

As history shows it, October 1929 was the date of the stock market crash that was the beginning of the Great Depression. Our records show that we were not affected as soon as some of the rest of the country by the Depression, and our sales improved in 1930 over 1929, as did our profits. We showed sales of $27,103.00 in 1930, and our profits rose to $2,103.04. This was too good to last however, and in 1931 and 1932 we were in the depths of the Depression and we were very close to insolvency during those years. Our total sales for 1932 were $14,293.72 and we showed a net loss for that year of $1,741.75.

As this is being written in the year of 1979, with inflation at full speed ahead, it is very difficult to see how it was possible to operate a plant, pay wages to support five families, pay the rent ($35.00 per month), buy the ingredients, (sugar A 3.25 cwt), buy the bottles and cases (bottles A 3.15 per gross), operate three trucks, etc., with a total income of only $14,293.72. Somehow we did, and with the help of our creditors, we managed to turn the corner in 1933 and our sales improved each year during 1934 and 1935. In 1935 we reached and exceeded our sales of 1930 and the records show that in 1935 we sold $30,641.78 worth of merchandise on which we made a profit of $2,513.83, which was a record profit up to that time.

Also during the Great Depression we managed to improve our public image by moving to more suitable quarters for the operation of a food plant. It was in 1931 that we bought a lot and built our own building to house our bottling business. For the lot on North Main Street we paid $1,719.40 and the building we erected on it cost $5,151.23. In order to do this we had to borrow $8,000.00 from the Bank of Marion. This paid for the building and lot and paid off the balance of the indebtedness of the original purchase. In order to secure this loan it was necessary to borrow some stocks from Mr. J.R. Shanklin, as collateral. Among the securities put up as

Original building built in 1930 & 1931 on North Main Street. This was our first home in our own property.

14

Bottling Machinery in use in the new plant in 1933. Shown is the Dixie Bottle Filler & Capper and the Meyer Dumore Jr. Bottle washing machine. Capacity of this machine was 24 six ounce bottles per minute.

collateral were 13 shares of the Bank of Bramwell, West Virginia. This stock was supposed to be worth $1,000.00 per share or more. The irony of the situation was that in 1932 the Bank of Bramwell closed its doors, never to reopen. The stockholders were subject to a double assessment and had to come up with an amount equal to the par value of their stock to help repay the depositors of the bank. Needless to say, this made the Bank of Marion very unhappy with their collateral, but as they did not know anything about operating a bottling plant, there was not much they could do about the circumstances. At any rate, in April 1931, the Marion Bottling Company opened its new bottling plant on North Main Street in a new building that was subsequently added to on eleven different occasions. This was to be the home of the company from 1931 to 1968 - a period of 37 years.

As the Depression continued to get worse and as money continued to be in short supply, it was increasingly hard to sell soft drinks. Many merchants wanted and needed to purchase soft drinks for their inventory, but could not find the money to do so. Almost all of our business was done on a cash basis as we could not possibly finance a line of credit to our customers. As a result, our sales touched bottom in 1932 when we were only able to sell about 18,000 cases for a total sales dollar volume of $14,293.72.

In 1931, in order to bolster our faltering sales, we decided to try selling what was known in those days as near beer. As prohibition was in effect, Anheuser-Busch bottled Budweiser and Bevo as non-alcoholic beverages or near beer and we secured the franchise to distribute them. In 1932 prohibition was repealed and we had the opportunity to secure the Anheuser-Busch franchise for their brand of beer. The Bank of Marion sent a committee to see us to advise that they thought we should secure a good brand of beer to distribute, as it appeared to them that the soft drink industry was doomed by the repeal of prohibition. When we questioned them about financing such a venture they declined as they said we already owed them too much. Nevertheless, we did sign a franchise agreement with Anheuser-Busch and ordered our first carload of beer. It was to be shipped on a sight draft, bill of lading attached, which meant that we had to remit $4,500.00 before we could unload the car. As the time approached we could see no way of raising $4,500.00, so, knowing that Mr. Beattie Gwyn, who was then operating Marion Ice & Coal Company, was very anxious to get in the beer business, we called him on the phone and offered to help transfer the franchise to him if he would take the car off our hands. This he gladly did, and thus, was born another business, The Gwyn Distributing Company. The company did later lose the Budweiser franchise, but switched to selling Schlitz beer which they continue to handle to this time.

In retrospect it was fortunate for us that we were unable to finance the beer business. Had we been able to finance the first car of beer we would probably have strained our financial position to the breaking point and thus not have been able to take advantage of opportunities in the soft drink business. The early years of the beer distributing business were extremely rough ones. Price cutting was extensive and many times beer was sold at less than cost in order to attract customers. All this was before the state stepped in with regulations that saved the industry from this ruinous competition.

In another effort to supplement our income, particularly in the winter time, we went into the retail coal business in 1930 and remained in that business till 1934. We built a coal tipple and coal yard on the lower end of Broadway to store our coal and we solicited business throughout the Town of Marion. This business was partially successful, as we were able to sell a good part of the coal in the town, and considering the fact that there were a number of other retail coal dealers. However, when the Marion & Rye Valley Railroad ceased operating a switching service, and sold their tracks and equipment, our coal yard was left without rail service. We discontinued business because our only recourse was to truck coal in, which we considered to be uneconomical. Therefore, in 1934 we discontinued the retail coal business.

Chapter V

When the company started its corporate life in 1929, the one franchise it held for a nationally known beverage was with the Orange Crush Company. This franchise gave to the company the exclusive right to bottle Orange Crush, Grape Crush and Lemon Crush in Smyth County, Washington County, Grayson County, portions of Russell County, Wythe County, and Bland County, and the city of Bristol, including a portion of Sullivan County, Tennessee. As a part of the original purchase agreement, B. Scott Sprinkle acquired the Orange Crush Company franchise for Pulaski County, Floyd County, Carroll County, Giles County, and portions of Bland County, Wythe County and Montgomery County, all in Virginia.

As the Depression continued to worsen and as the bottling business continued to get more difficult, the Pulaski operation of Mr. Sprinkle likewise became unprofitable and appeared to be headed for bankruptcy. Mr Sprinkle wanted to dispose of his business and as we at Marion Orange Crush Bottling Company desperately needed more volume in order to survive, on December 9th, 1932 we completed an agreement with Mr. Sprinkle to take over his operation and to receive the Orange Crush franchise for the territory he served. Apparently, we did not regard this acquisition as very important as no record of the transaction was made in the minutes of the meetings of the board of directors or stockholders. A copy of the contract with Mr. Sprinkle reveals that Marion Orange Crush Bottling Company agreed to buy Mr. Sprinkle's bottles and cases. The company paid 85 cents for 24 bottles and the wooden case that contained the bottles. Where the bottles and cases were in the hands of customers there was an agreement that a deposit would be refunded to the customer. This deposit would then be deducted from the 85 cents paid to the company. Also, the Marion Company

We discovered that the bottling business has its ups & downs. This pictures a disastrous truck wreck we experienced in 1938 and which eventually brought a lawsuit which we lost to the tune of $18,000.00.

purchased ale extracts, syrups, crowns, etc., that were usable at market prices.

Mr. Sprinkle agreed to assign the Orange Crush Franchise to Marion Orange Crush Bottling Company, and to refrain from going into the soft drink business within the 'above territory for a period of two years.

Payment for the inventory was arranged so that $500.00 would be paid upon completion of the listing and pricing of the inventory with the balance at $100.00 per month until paid. This was an indication that not much cash was available in those days. Thus we acquired a considerable part of our presently franchised territory for very little investment.

When we started in business our best selling drink was Orange Crush. While we had a franchise for Grape Crush our predecessors had been bottling, and we continued to bottle, a grape drink called Good Grape. This was a product of Seminole Flavor Company of Chattanooga, Tennessee. We did bottle Lemon Crush, but the sales were indeed small. We were also bottling a chocolate drink made by the Orange Crush Company, as well as, a strawberry drink and a cherry drink. Also, we bottled a ginger ale which was a trade-mark registered drink by Sprinkle and Robinson as Blue Ridge Ginger Ale. This drink was bottled for many years, and was discontinued in the early 1970's due to the difficulty of obtaining private bottles in small quantities.

In our search for some way to increase our volume of business it became apparent early in our existence that a large percentage of the soft drink business was going to the cola flavor. Coca-Cola was the overpowering leader in the field, and the surveys we made by collection, and counting bottle tops from the stores we worked, showed that Coca-Cola was selling more than 60% of all beverages sold. Therefore, it became evident that if we were to compete we needed to have a cola drink.

Accordingly, we looked over all the then known brands and decided we liked the name Pepsi-Cola better than any other available. Therefore, on February 14th, 1929 we signed a franchise to bottle Pepsi-Cola. The agreement was with the parent company, National Pepsi-Cola Corporation of Richmond. This was the second time Pepsi-Cola had been sold in Marion, as the Sprinkle & Robinson partnership had previously bottled Pepsi-Cola in 1925. It is not known why it was discontinued at that time. After Marion Orange Crush Bottling Company had been bottling Pepsi-Cola for a little over a year the parent company, The National Pepsi-Cola Corporation went bankrupt and ceased operations, thus eliminating our source of supply. This happened on June 8th, 1931, and again, Marion Orange Crush Bottling Company found itself without a cola drink to bottle. We tried to fill the need by bottling a drink called Hi Peak Cola - it didn't sell, then we tried Braser - it didn't sell either. Try as much as we could we were unable to find anything that would compete in the cola market. Therefore, we were forced to rely on Orange Crush as our leading seller and be content to let the bulk of the business go to our giant competitor - Coca-Cola.

While we were experimenting with various cola drinks many things were happening to our former cola drink, Pepsi-Cola. A sale through the bankruptcy court in Richmond had been made to Roy C. Megargel of New York of the trade-mark, formula, and good will of Pepsi-Cola. Megargel, in turn, was financed by Charles G. Guth, who in turn, was financed by Loft Incorporated, a chain of candy stores. Guth was president of Loft Incorporated. It is recorded that the price paid was $10,500. The story of the manipulations of the ownership of Pepsi-Cola is a story in itself and we will not repeat it here. It is enough to say that the formula was worked on and improved by the New York ownership, and that the new Pepsi-Cola replaced Coca-Cola in the several hundred soda fountains in the candy stores owned by Loft Incorporated.

After finding that Pepsi-Cola sold well in the soda fountains, Mr. Guth and his newly organized Pepsi-Cola Company decided to bottle the drink, and they did so in a 6 oz. bottle. The result - most unimpressive. Then, they tried selling it in a 12 oz. bottle to retail for 10¢. Again, sales were negligible. Then, someone thought of selling the same product in a 12 oz. bottle for 5¢ retail. It was instant success and the New York market took to Pepsi-Cola in a big way. This new found success now enabled Pepsi-Cola to become a candidate for national distribution.

In early 1935 we were approached with a proposition to bottle Pepsi-Cola in a 12 oz. bottle by Mr. Joe LaPides, owner of the Surburban Club Bottling Company of Baltimore, the bottler of Pepsi-Cola in Baltimore, and also, the representative of the Pepsi-Cola Company for the eastern part of the United States. We turned him down, and told him we had already tried Pepsi-Cola with only a very small degree of success. Further, that we did not believe that any drink produced in a 12 oz. bottle to sell at 5¢ retail could be of the quality that we wanted to sell.

Later that year we heard stories from places like Winston-Salem, N. C., Lynchburg, Va., and Norfolk, Va. of what a fantastic job Pepsi-Cola was doing in those places. The writer got in his car and went to Winston-Salem to talk to Mr. Van Melchor, the Orange Crush bottler and, the newly franchised Pepsi-Cola bottler. Mr. Melchor was enthusiastic about Pepsi-Cola.

That fall the Convention of the American Bottlers of Carbonated Beverages was held in Baltimore. The writer attended that convention and talked with numerous Orange Crush bottlers, some of whom had taken on Pepsi-Cola. All of those were enjoying huge successes in bottling Pepsi-Cola. It was then, that the writer swallowed his pride, and hunted up Mr. LaPides to ask if the franchise for Pepsi-Cola was still open for the territory we covered.

Mr. LaPides said that the territory was still open, and that he would like us to have it, but that Mr. Guth had taken the issuance of franchises out of his hands. Now, all prospective bottlers of Pepsi-Cola had to go to New York, and personally interview with Mr. Guth. If he approved of them a franchise would be offered. Mr. LaPides agreed to make an appointment with Mr. Guth to interview the writer in New York, and shortly afterward, notified us that Mr. Guth would see us on December 8th, 1935.

Therefore, on December 6th the writer departed by train for New York to keep the appointment with Mr. Guth of the Pepsi-Cola Company. Never having been to New York before, and being from a small town, the writer was very much awed and out of place in this big city. A room was obtained at the old Pennsylvania Hotel, just across the street from the Pennsylvania Station, and as I recall it, the room rate was $2.50 per day. A rather high rate for one used to paying $1.00 to $2.00 for rooms in hotels. Anyway, on the appointed day, and at the appointed time, the writer showed up at the Pepsi-Cola Company plant and office which was then located in an old factory building on 33rd street in Queens.

I presented myself to Mr. Guth's secretary, a man named McHurin, who in turn, turned me over to first one individual and then another. These people obviously were attempting to pump enthusiam into the prospective bottler before his conference with the "great man" himself, Mr. Guth. This did not go so well with the writer, as he sensed that the whole thing was a propaganda session, and that the actors in the thing were discounting the intelligence of the prospective bottler. So when the writer was finally allowed to see Mr. Guth the mood was not exactly what it had been intended to be.

Finally about 2 p.m., after having been passed from one person to another since the 10 a.m. appointment time, I was shown into Mr. Guth's office. Mr. Guth was seated at the end of a very long conference table and at the time was talking over two telephones, alternately, and continued to do so for several minutes. I stood at the other end of the table, nervously shifting my weight from foot to foot and holding my coat over my arm and my hat in hand. Finally, Mr. Guth slammed down the phones and turned to me and opened the conversation by saying, "Well, what do you want?"

I introduced myself and told him I had been sent to see him by Mr. Joe LaPides with regard to securing a franchise to bottle Pepsi-Cola. Mr. Guth said, "Well, will you throw out that other 'junk' you are bottling and bottle Pepsi-Cola alone?"

I answered that I could not and would not agree to that as I had been able to make a living out of the products I had, and was unwilling to discontinue bottling them. I told him I would, however, agree to taking on Pepsi-Cola and promoting it to the best of my ability.

Mr. Guth then replied, "Well, you are not enthusiastic enough about Pepsi-Cola. We want enthusiastic bottlers for Pepsi-Cola."

By that time, I had had it. I felt that I was being put through some sort of inquisition, and that Mr. Guth, and his associates, were of the opinion that they could force me to do anything they wanted me to do. So I jammed my hat down on my head and told Mr. Guth that I was very sorry to have wasted his time as well as my own in coming to New York. With that I strode out of the office loudly slamming the door as I left. I have seldom been as angry as I was at that time.

Mr. Guth's secretary, a Mr. Chester McHurin had his desk outside of Mr. Guth's office. He followed me out trying to pacify me and he followed me clear to the street entrance. As I had to get Mr. McHurin to call me a taxi I was forced to talk to him. After a cooling off period Mr. McHurin persuaded me to go back to his desk so that he could call a cab for me. Once there he told me Mr. Guth had changed his mind and wanted me as a bottler. He then produced a franchise form already signed by Mr. Guth and I handed him a check for $315.00 for one unit of Pepsi-Cola. A unit included syrup, crowns and labels sufficient to bottle 1,200 cases of Pepsi-Cola.

And so we entered the Pepsi-Cola business.

The years of 1936 to 1942 were the fastest growth period of our entire history. Case sales increased 147% in 1936 over 1935, 43% in 1937 over 1936, 16% in 1938 over 1937, 19% in 1939 over 1938, 10% in 10 months of 1940 (we changed our fiscal year at this time to close on October 31st) over 1939, and a whopping 48% in 1941 over the 10 month period of 1940. These startling and sensational increases were achieved on account of the sales success of Pepsi-Cola.

Our building on North Main Street after the addition and remodeling of 1938.

Chapter VI

We started out bottling Pepsi-Cola in any kind of a 12 oz. bottle we could lay our hands on - green, brown, white or any shade in between. Likewise, the shape of the bottle did not matter, water shape, beer bottle shape or ketchup bottle shape did not matter. All we were required to do was furnish a 12 oz. bottle and paste on it the Pepsi-Cola label. We bought many truckloads of green Cananda Dry and White Rock bottles from a junk yard in Camden, New Jersey. These had been collected over the years from the hotels and bars at Atlantic City.

For cases we used a full depth wooden case that was made in Pepsi-Cola's own box factory in New York. We bought them at a price of 28¢ each, delivered. We, of course, had to provide cardboard dividers to insert in these wooden boxes to prevent bottle breakage. This supply of cheap bottles and cases helped us to expand our business as fast as we did, because had we been required to use new bottles, and buy our cases from the regular suppliers, the cash outlay would have been quite an obstacle. It was estimated in those days that a bottler had to buy 4 cases of bottles for each additional case sold.

Bottles and cases provided one problem for a rapidly growing business, but not the only one by any means. Trucks had to be provided to handle the additional business. In 1936 we had three route trucks, and one extra truck which was used part-time to haul coal for the coal business. In 1938 our fleet of trucks had grown to ten route trucks and one pickup.

Our case sales in 1935 were 37,643 while our case sales in 1941 amounted to 497,613, an increase of more than 13 times our volume for 1935. In addition to bottles and cases, trucks and other delivery vehicles, it was also necessary to re-equip with bottling equipment to handle the added volume. We started the six year period with a Dixie Bottling machine with a top speed of 24 bottles per minute. We replaced that machine with a Liquid Carbonic Corporation Red Diamond 12 spout machine with a 30 bottle per minute capacity. This was, in turn, replaced with a Red Diamond 18 spout machine with a bottle capacity of 48 bottles per minute. This machine was also too small, and in November 1941, we placed an order for a Liquid Carbonic low pressure 40 spout machine with a capacity of 130 bottles per minute. Of course, bottle washing equipment, labeling machine, carbonators and other bottling equipment had to be obtained to match the filling equipment.

We outgrew our bottling plant room, and we purchased the furniture store building adjoining our bottling plant. We bridged and covered the space between the buildings, and used the newly acquired building for storage. Then, in 1941, we embarked on a building program which completely remodeled the furniture store addition, and added new construction, to the west of that building. This construction was done by Eubank & Caldwell, a Roanoke firm of architects and contractors at a final cost of around $35,000. This seemed to us at the time to be an enormous sum, but, of course, now it seems to have been a great bargain.

The six year period we have been discussing was one in which great effort was expended and good results were obtained in improving our competitive standing in the market place. We were most fortunate to have, during this period, a group of dedicated, industrious and expert sales people in our organization. At the beginning of the period there were many locations from which we were excluded. Our chief competition, Coca-Cola, had continually, and often successfully, drilled into the thinking of the store owners, the idea that they could not do without Coca-Cola while they could do without other soft drinks. This thinking, plus the fact that Pepsi-Cola had paper labels that came off in the then prevalent wet bath bottle coolers (the newest thing in refrigeration at that time) or in the old ice boxes, made selling

Sales & Delivery Personnel 1938 & Fleet of Trucks
Left to Right: E. N. Legard, Kyle O. Helton, W. S. McClellan, Paul E. Houston, Wiley E. Webb, William T. Legard, H. D. McClellan, Maiden Romans, C. L. Roland, C. W. Legard.

a very difficult thing. Many times when we thought we had things going fine for us at an outlet, we would drive up and find our empties stacked up with orders to pick them up and refund the deposit. This was most discouraging, and had we had people with less tenacity and fortitude than Ned Legard, Kyle Helton, Shular McClellan, Earl Webb, Harse McClellan and others, we could never have had the success which we did achieve. At the end of the period we had not overtaken our chief competitor, but we were in a strong second place and were beginning to think that eventually it might just be possible for us to claim we were number one.

The years 1942 to 1947 were the War Years. In December 1941, war suddenly became a reality. Even though we vaguely expected it to happen, it broke on us suddenly, and we were very much unprepared for it. However, we were lucky in some ways, and much of our later success was due to the decisions and actions made and undertaken during the period of rationing and restrictions.

To begin with we had purchased a large quantity of sugar in the fall of 1941, and had stored it in the Rhea Building. Our thinking was that we would have trouble being able to secure sugar, should war come; also we needed to protect ourselves against a price increase. One of the first actions the government took was to sieze all supplies of sugar and to freeze the price of sugar at $5.80 per cwt. Our supply of sugar did not benefit us at all, except to give us peace of mind as to where the sugar the government allowed us to use, was to come from - out of our own stock.

By January, 1942, we were under full sugar rationing which started at 70% of the amount of sugar used in the corresponding month of the year 1941. The amount varied from month to month and later quotas ranged from a low of 50% of the amount used in the same period of 1941, to a high of 90% of that amount. Therefore, we were obliged to ration our customers on the same ratio as we were able to produce our products. At the same time, the market overnight became a seller's market and it was no problem at all to sell all we could produce.

Sugar, was by no means, all our troubles, as crowns or bottle tops were also a very serious limiting factor. In fact at times it was possible to get an allowance of sugar that would make more bottles of soft drinks than we had crowns to close them with. This was due to the demands for tinplate used for crowns and the shortage of cork which at that time was the exclusive liner used in soft drink closures. We partially overcame the tinplate shortage by going to the various industrial users of large size food cans, like the Southwestern State Hospital, and reclaiming their used tin cans. These we brought to the plant, cut the ends out, sliced the body of the can open, cut out the seam, flattened out the metal, washed it, packaged it in crates, and shipped it to the crown manufacturers who in turn made it into crowns for us. Thus, we were able to supplement our crown allotment to make a few more cases.

Also, in order to survive, we used reclaimed crowns. As our salesmen made their rounds they solicited the used crowns they found in the stores and other outlets where soft drinks were sold. These crowns were boxed up and sent to certain crown manufacturers to be reworked. They were stripped of their cork liners and paint; then the crowns were reformed, finished with a coat of lacquer, a new cork liner, and returned to us. Our records show that in 1942 and 1943 approximately 10% of our total production was with the use of reclaimed crowns.

Gasoline was severely rationed, and we were forced to conserve gasoline to an extent we did not think possible at the time. By appealing to the rationing board, we were able to get some relief on our gasoline allottment.

Tires were another very vital item that was almost unobtainable, especially in the larger sizes. We finally located a set of tires for our one tractor-trailer we owned, bought them on the black market at an outrageous price, and made them do for the duration.

Machine parts were also practically unobtainable. Therefore, when we had a breakdown, it became necessary for us to fix whatever was broken or worn out. This we did by using our own shop or getting what help we could from local machine shops. Mr. C. W. Richardson, who operated a machine shop out the street a short distance from our plant, was a friend indeed at this time.

By using every method we could think of, we managed to hold our production through the war years, 1941-1946, at about 100% of the prewar years. As a result of shortages of materials, a strong seller's market existed. Our sales were limited only by the amount of soft drinks we could produce. Early in this seller's market we insititued a rationing system for our customers. We did a very good job of providing an even distribution of our products to our customers. Most of our competitors did not bother with a rationing system, and simply sold all their production as close to their bottling plants as they could, thus leaving customers in distant parts of the territory to do without. After the war, when restrictions were lifted, we were in excellent position to benefit from the trouble we were put to in maintaining a rationing system. Our customers felt we had treated them fairly and that most of our competitors had failed to do so. Consequently, our sales in 1946 were 690,644 cases, as against 497,613 in 1941. Another very beneficial asset we enjoyed from our rationing days was that many of our customers had been so brainwashed by our chief competitor, Coca-Cola, that they thought it would be impossible to stay in business without Coca-Cola. By their failure to furnish any Coca-Cola to many of their customers, the myth of power of Coca-Cola was dispelled. The merchants realized that Pepsi-Cola was able to compete favorably with what had been previously considered the overwhelming favorite single drink in the whole beverage field.

Another plus for our company that came out of the adversities we went through during the war years was that it enabled us to get our "toe in the door" in the soda fountain business, and later in the post mix business. At the beginning of the war Coca-Cola ruled supreme in the cola syrup sales. The parent Coca-Cola Company sold all fountain outlets and they almost had a monopoly on that phase of the business. As the war progressed, they had to severely ration their outlets because of the sugar rationing. Consequently, the fountain operators were most receptive to any additional source of syrup. The Coca-Cola Company owned most of the dispensing equipment in the outlets, and of course, refused to let the fountain operators use their equipment for any other syrup. This created a problem for their competitors as no such equipment could be had at that time. Pepsi-Cola, however, promoted the idea of bottling the Pepsi-Cola syrup in bottles and using fiber or cardboard stoppers in the bottles, as crowns were unavailable. These bottles of syrup were sold to fountain operators who measured the correct amount of syrup into a glass, added ice and carbonated water from their fountains, and produced a fountain Pepsi-Cola. We entered the fountain syrup business of Pepsi-Cola during the war years, and when the war ended we found ourselves in a much better position to face stiff competition, than if we had waited until after the war to try to enter this field.

As stated before, we ended the war years with greater annual sales than at the beginning of these troubled years. We also entered the fountain syrup business during this time. All this took sugar, and sugar was rationed throughout the period at as low as 50% of 1941 usage, and up to 90% on occasion. How did we accomplish this? Well, to begin with, during the base year we were bottling most all of our beverages in 12 oz. bottles. We were selling a lot of Milkay Orange and Mandalay Punch in 12 oz. bottles. These and other flavors in the 12 oz. bottles were discontinued. We used the sugar this saved in

Orange Crush in a 7 oz. bottle, and in Blue Ridge Ginger Ale also in a 7 oz. bottle.

Pepsi-Cola, early in the war years, managed to beat Coca-Cola to the punch and secured all the Mexican surplus sugar crop. This could not be imported into this country as sugar, but there was nothing in the laws or regulations to prevent the importation of bottle flavoring syrup. Therefore, the Pepsi-Cola Company set up a syrup plant in Monterray, Mexico, which made a heavy sugar syrup, added a little acid and sugar coloring, and called it El Masco. This was then shipped into the United States by rail car shipments.

We were able to talk Pepsi-Cola into letting us have a substantial amount of this syrup to put into Pepsi-Cola and Pepsi-Cola fountian syrup. Also, due to the fact that we had placed an order for machinery to give us added capacity, and this coincided with the time slot that the rationing laws allowed for an additional sugar allottment, we got sugar over our quota. All of these things combined with a fortunate purchase of two car-loads of wheat sugar to enable us to produce at a rate of more than 100% of our 1941 production and to come through the difficult war years in a good competitive position.

Chapter VII

The post-war period of 1945 to 1955 were years of great importance in which many adjustments and changes were made at Marion Bottling Company. They were years in which developments that vitally affected the future of our industry were brought about. It was a time in which Pepsi-Cola, our star performer, touched rock bottom and then began to rise again. They were years in which plans were developed in our company that have served us well in subsequent years.

From the beginning of the soft drink industry in the eighteen hundreds to the post World War II years the traditional selling price of a soft drink, be it a bottled or a fountain drink, was five cents. Coca-Cola, Pepsi-Cola, Orange Crush, Green River, Chero-Cola, Cherry Smash, Smile, and all the rest of the old timers were advertised to sell for 5¢. The price was advertised almost as much as the beverage. The merchants, as well as, the public simply regarded the 5¢ selling price of soft drinks as a way of life and, as such, something that could not be changed.

During the war years, the prices of sugar, wages, and most other costs were frozen. The price of sugar for instance remained at $5.80 per cwt for the entire time between 1941 and 1946. After 1946 controls on material and wages were gradually removed and prices then began to increase. Our costs increased also when this happened, but our selling price remained the same. There was no place for the increase in costs to come from except from our profits. It appeared that soon profits would disappear entirely as we operated on a very close margin, and did not have much room to absorb increased costs. Therefore, in 1947 we decided that we would try to get an increased price for our products. Our local competing bottlers had been complaining about their deteriorating financial position, and we thought if we would lead off with a price increase they would follow. Therefore, we announced, and put in effect, a price increase of 16 cents per case in the wholesale price of our products. Instead of following our example, our competitiors used the fact that we had increased our price as a selling weapon against us. As a result, after holding our 96¢ price for 7 months we began to lose customers in increasing numbers, and subsequently, we were forced to retreat to our old price of 80¢ per case.

This left us with no alternative except to cut expenses to the very lowest possible position and to determine to ride out the storm until our competition felt enough economic pressure to increase their price. This we did, and in 1951, the Coca-Cola Bottling Company of Roanoke announced a price increase to 96¢ per case. As soon as we heard the news we called in our trucks operating in the territory, covered jointly with the Roanoke company, and sent them back out the same day with our price up to 96¢ also. Thus, we advertised the fact that we would support a price increase in any portion of our territory where our chief competition would go up. Roanoke covered only about 30% of our territory and it was 1955 before we succeeded in getting all of our territory to break out of the traditional selling price of 5¢, and go to what was then the selling price of 6¢ per bottle. The extra 16¢ per case enabled us to pass on the increasing costs of labor to the consumer and thus realize a reasonable profit. Since the original break through of the price barrier of 5¢ we have had over a period of many years several advances in prices. None of these price increases have met with anything like the resistance from the merchants, and also from the public, that we experienced back in the fifties when we struggled to a selling price of 6¢.

In the late 1940's Pepsi-Cola, which by that time was the star performer in our list of soft drinks, suffered decreases in sales on a national level. The parent company not only lost sales, but their profits declined and this and other factors resulted in discouragement and disunity among Pepsi-Cola bottlers. Walter S. Mack, who was President and Chairman of the Board of Pepsi-Cola Company, was accused by many Pepsi-Cola bottlers of being more interested in manipulation of the stock of Pepsi-Cola on the stock exchange than in pushing the sale of Pepsi-Cola. One of the bad moves Mr. Mack made in the late 40's was to contract with the Hupp Corporation for a large number of vending machines which were subsequently sold to Pepsi-Cola bottlers, of whom we were one. We bought a number of these machines for our initial entry into the vending market and they were a dismal failure. We were never able to get any reasonable service from the Hupp machines. Additionally, we were in competition with Coca-Cola and their machines always proved superior to ours. Consequently, we lost business, and in many cases, customers on account of Mr. Mack's purchase of untested and unwarranted machines. All of these things caused Pepsi-Cola to reach a new low in sales and profits by 1950.

In 1950 Mr. Mack was removed as Chief Operating Officer and Mr. Al Steele was brought in. Mr. Steele was exactly what the Pepsi-Cola Company needed at the time. He restored the bottlers' confidence in Pepsi-Cola by several bold and radical moves, and started the parent company back on the road to increased sales and profits. That is a long and interesting story in itself, but too long to be told here. However, it is only fair to say that the prosperity of the Pepsi-Cola Company was certainly tied in with our corresponding increase in sales and profits.

It was in the decade we are discussing that we really decided to go after, in a big way, the problem of a lack of refrigeration in the area. Before World War II we had sold a variety of refrigeration equipment, ice boxes, wet bath electric coolers, etc. None of these were completely satisfactory to the users of the equipment. About the time the war started we sold a few "dry" coolers to our dealers. These proved very satisfactory, but the war soon shut off our supply. As the war wound down our dealers were in a buying mood, and we took advantage of that fact by taking orders with down payments for coolers to be delivered as soon as they were available. We were very successful and at one time had orders in hand together with cash deposits for more than 300 electric bottlers coolers. Altogether we sold more than 1,000 electric bottle coolers over a two or three year period. When these were finally delivered our soft drink sales responded favorably in the on-premise market.

It was also in this period that we recovered from our initial failure in the vending market and decided to go after the vending market seriously. In 1955 we placed our first carload order for vending machines after cautiously trying out the machines to see that they could be made to work. We bought this carload from Vendolator Company which was about the only vending machine manufacturer that was not tied up with an exclusive contract with the Coca-Cola Company. Their machines were indeed not perfect, but they did perform well enough that we became a factor in the vending market and gave us the satisfaction of being able to give battle to our big competitor.

It was in 1950 just after Mr. Steele was made President of Pepsi-Cola Company that he allowed bottlers of Pepsi-Cola to change from the 12 oz. size bottle to a 10 oz. bottle. This was a change we had wanted for several years as it allowed us to compete on approximately an even cost basis with Coca-Cola. At 12 ounces our costs per case were in excess of those of Coca-Cola in their 6 1/2 oz. bottle. Consequently, they were able to spend much more on such marketing tools as advertising and merchandising. In 1948 or 1949 the writer, along with Mr. Herbert Thomas of the Pepsi-Cola Bottling Company of Winston-Salem, N.C., made a trip to New York and had an audience with Mr. Walter Mack of Pepsi-Cola Company. Our intent was to point this fact out, and urge him to release the franchise restricting our bottle sizes so that we would be able to use a 9 oz. or 10 oz. bottle, and thereby, be in a better competitive position. After hearing us out, Mr. Mack told us, in a polite way, of course, that the bottle size was no business of ours, and that we should return home and mind our own business. I well remember a statement he made at the time. He said, "Pepsi-Cola may be sold at a price of 80¢ per case, 96¢ per case or $1.20 per case, but it will never be sold in any size bottle but a 12 oz. size." In the light of the present day proliferation of bottle sizes this statement shows how short our foresight is sometimes. Later, Mr. Steele (Mr. Mack's successor) showed good judgement as well as a lot of courage to allow a reduction in bottle size at a time when the financial picture of Pepsi-Cola Company was rather dark. Such a reduction in bottle size meant a reduction in the sales of syrup that the Pepsi-Cola Company furnished, for the same number of cases produced. However, he soon found out that the change allowed the bottlers to advertise and merchandise more and thereby created an increased demand for Pepsi-Cola syrup, thereby increasing the amount of syrup sold.

This was true in our case. In 1950 we began buying 10 oz. bottles and started converting our territory, area by area, to the 10 oz. package. We found that the public accepted the bottle with favor, and the additional revenue we received put us in a much better position to advertise and merchandise. Sales increased each year from 1948 to 1955, with the largest yearly increases being after the 10 oz. bottle was introduced. In fact, our total sales in 1955 were more than double our sales in 1945. Our sales of Pepsi-Cola alone increased from 440,000 cases in 1945 to 1,012,000 cases in 1955, more than double in the 10 year period. Increased sales required more employees to handle the added sales. Our number of employees increased from 47 people in 1945 to 90 people in 1955.

To celebrate this fact, and to acknowledge that we had achieved a per capita level of 100 bottles per person per year in our territory, as well as establishing a volume of more than

The dinner party held in 1956 at Holston Hills Country Club to celebrate our sales successes of 1955 when we exceeded 100 Bottles per capitia of Pepsi-Cola in our franchised territory.

Pictured seated at table L to R: W. M. HULL, JR.; DON KENDALL (now Chairman of Pepsi-Co, Inc.); FRED BERGRIN, District Manager of Pepsi-Cola, Washington Region; DICK BURGESS, Vice President-Sales, Pepsi-Cola Co.; CARL SALTS, Divisional Vice President, Pepsi-Cola Co. (Standing at mike:) JOE LAPIDES, Baltimore, Md.

1,000,000 cases annually, we held a celebration party at Holston Hills Country Club. Our entire organization was invited as well as many suppliers and friends. We were presented awards from the Pepsi-Cola Company, who sent a distinguished group of officials to make the presentation. Among this group were long time friend Joe LaPides, and a rather newcomer to the organization, Donald M. Kendall, who was destined to become President and the Chairman of Pepsi Company, Inc. Mr. Kendall at the time of our party in 1956 was Vice President in charge of national accounts and syrup sales of Pepsi-Cola Company.

It was in this ten year peiod that we made several definite decisions that affected our future growth. One of the most important of these decisions was to resist the urgings of the Pepsi-Cola Company to break the territory into three franchises and establish plants in each of these areas. They brought considerable pressure on us to put plants in Pulaski and Bristol as well as retain the one in Marion. It was their position then that multiple small plants resulted in more sales than a central plant with warehouses. We disagreed with them and definitely decided to develop our distribution system around a central plant with warehouses, where distances dictated. We stuck to our decision and the Pepsi-Cola Company in later years reversed their thinking entirely to correspond with ours.

Also, it was during this time that we evolved our system of controls on our warehouse operations. Many bottlers became disenchanted with the warehouse system because of bad experience in the area of operations of the warehouses. We have never had any really serious losses or foul ups with our system.

Likewise we began to make plans to upgrade our warehouse facilities. Up to 1955 we made out with very inadequate warehouse facilities. In Bristol, for instance, we had bought an old store building on Massachusetts Avenue which we used as a warehouse. Although we added a small addition to the rear of the old store, it would neither hold enough of our products nor would it store all of our trucks. The loading and unloading was done by hand, using roller conveyers, which was most inefficient as well as laborious. In 1955 we purchased a good location on the eastern approach to the city. We later erected a very adequate building especially constructed for warehouse use. We also began to look for better locations to erect our own buildings in Pulaski, Hillsville, and Galax. Lebanon was served from a building we erected in 1946, which was our first adventure in constructing a warehouse. We learned from it many things not to do in the building of future warehouses. Later, when we decided to build in Bristol we corrected many of the errors we made in the old Lebanon setup and developed a basic plan that we have followed in later construction. This has proven to be a very efficient plan for handling our products for these many years.

Chapter VIII

The ten year period 1955 to 1965 was a period in our history that was notable as a time in which we steadily marched ahead without much change in products manufactured or methods of operation. It was a period of progress, but lacking in spectacular moves either in methods of doing business or in advertising and merchandising. It was a period in which we continued to increase our ability to make a profit, as well as in which we accumulated more capital for use in the future years. It was a period in which we improved management staff, and further trained and educated all our employees in their jobs.

After our break through of the 5¢ price barrier was accomplished, in 1955, we were able in the succeeding ten-year period to advance our average selling price per case and better keep up with the advancing costs of production. In 1955, for instance, our average selling price was 90¢ per case. In 1956 it advanced to 99¢ per case. In 1957 it was $1.05 per case, and each succeeding year it increased until by 1965 our average selling price had reached $1.34 per case.

The retail price that our beverages were sold for likewise steadily advanced from the 6¢ price that was instituted in 1955, until by 1965, the majority of our products were being sold for 10¢ per bottle. Thus, the dealer maintained his margin of profit, and in most cases, improved it during the ten-year period. This gave him added incentive to push the sale of soft drinks, which resulted in better displays and stocks in the stores. Additionally, it caused increased unit sales in spite of higher prices.

Our sales in 1955 totalled 1,195,544 cases. Almost all of these cases were in the 10 oz. package, with probably less than 1%, in the 8 oz. size bottle. By 1965 the comparable figures were 1,480,692 cases sold, all of it being in the 10 oz. package. Sales in dollars increased from barely over $1,000,000.00 in

1955 to almost $2,000,000.00 in 1965 because of the increased selling price.

As far as products manufactured and sold were concerned the only notable change came in 1965 when we began bottling and selling Mountain Dew. In that year we sold 184,000 cases which made it our second best seller, exceeded only by Pepsi-Cola.

Probably the most important thing accomplished during the period under discussion was the addition of personnel to our staff that had much to do with the future successes of the company. Many of our fine group of employees who joined us during these ten years became loyal and devoted workers to whom much credit is due for the successful and profitable years that followed. It would be impossible for me to name all of these persons, so I will have to confine my credits to those who became officers of the company at a later date. These included I. Hugh Slagle, who joined us in 1957, and Preston S. Copenhaver, Jr., who joined us in 1962. Mr. Slagle joined the company after graduating from Virginia Tech with a degree in Business Administration. He had previously worked in our office before joining the Air Force and later attending college. He brought to us a much needed updating on our accounting procedures, and he assumed charge of the office management of the company.

Mr. Copenhaver joined us in 1962 after completing his college requirements and receiving a B.S. degree at V.P.I. He subsequently studied and earned his Masters Degree in Chemical Engineering from the same institution. After a six-year stay with Texas Eastman Corporation in Longview, Texas where he was rapidly promoted, he brought to us knowledge and expertise that fit perfectly into our organization. He first was assigned the position as sales manager where he distinguished himself in the performance of duties which he claimed to be the least fitted for.

Thus, during this period of ten years, our organizational chart began to take a form that was to provide for the future expansion and growth of Marion Bottling Company. Also during the same period of time we initiated plans for the physical expansion of our manufacturing facilities. We began to realize during the early ninteen sixties that we were falling behind in the competitive race for first place in the market place by not being able to compete with any new package size that was being offered to the public. Our machinery would not handle any larger package than the 12 oz. bottle. In other markets the 16 oz. bottle was beginning to sell in volume. Coca-Cola was offering a quart size in many markets with success. We found that space requirement for larger machinery to handle larger sizes was not to be had in our old building, and the lot at that location did not permit any more additions to our old building. Therefore, we began to try to find a location on which to erect a new plant to house machinery that would permit us to better meet the demand for additional package sizes.

Our first selection was to acquire a lot in the newly developed industrial park. We did buy a lot there, where the plant of American Furniture Company is now located, but after considering the poor access to the interstate highway, and the fact that we did not like being located near some other industries that might detract from the image of cleanliness and wholesomeness that a food product should have, we decided to sell our acreage and look elsewhere. This we did, and finally settled on our present site, which has proven to be a very excellent location. We bought this site in 1965, and started planning for bigger and better facilities for the years to come.

So it was that the 1955-1965 period, a period in which nothing much spectacular happened in sales volume, methods of operation, or distinct changes of products, became a period of preparation for bigger things. It was also a period of accumulation of capital with which we were able to accomplish these larger goals in successive years.

Chapter IX

We mentioned in the previous chapter that we began bottling Mountain Dew in 1965. This very fine beverage quickly gained, and steadily maintained the number two sales position since its development. We will digress here to recount the history of that drink, which is a native of our own town of Marion, Virginia. Mountain Dew was created, and started by, The Tip Corporation of America. The Tip Corporation of American was originated by Clay F. Church, then President of the Dr Pepper Bottling Company of Marion. The corporation was founded for the purpose of marketing and selling a grape flavored drink named Tip. This drink, and the copyrighted name, was purchased by Mr. Church from Gary Beverage Company of Charlotte, N. C., and was to be marketed and sold in a manner similar to a very good seller in its day known as Grapette. Just as this corporation, The Tip Corporation, began to function, World War II came on and the drink did not succeed well, and later on faded completely out.

About 1945 or 1946, Mr. Church employed W. H. Jones as manager of The Tip Corporation. Mr. Jones was then a salesman for National Fruit Flavor Company, and sold their line of bottle flavoring extracts in this area. When he took over the Tip Corporation he found it heavily in debt, and loaded down with promises and commitments that could not be kept. Consequently, he was not able to stem the decline of sales of the main product of the company, the drink Tip. Consequently, after Mr. Church's personal and business affairs forced him to take bankrupty, Mr. Jones found himself with a corporation that could not meet its obligations. Two stockholders who had been brought into the organization, and had signed notes of several thousand dollars were unhappy and offered to give their stock to anyone who would relieve them of their obligations on account of the endorsed notes. Thereupon Mr. Jones set about to refinance the Tip Corporation. He solicited help from several of his old customers while he was selling flavors for the National Fruit Flavor Corporation. He did secure five people who agreed to put $1,500.00 apiece into his corporation in exchange for stock. The five persons who refinanced the Tip Corporation was Allie Hartman, of Knoxville, Tenn., Herman Minges of Lumberton, N. C., Richard Minges of Fayetteville, N. C., Wythe M. Hull, Jr. of Marion, Virginia and W. H. Jones of Marion, Virginia. The proceeds of the sale of stock in the corporation paid off the notes against the Tip Corporation and left a modest amount of operating funds for the company.

The intention of the new stockholders was to market Tip as best they could, and to add other flavors until a full line of flavors could be offered for sale. At one of the first meetings held by the directors of the newly organized company, Mr. Hartman of Knoxville stated that he and his brother, W. Barney Hartman, owned the trade-mark of a lemon-lime type drink that they called Mountain Dew. They had not developed it in any way except to bottle it as a mixer for their personal entertaining and they would be glad to donate it to the Tip Corporation if Mr. Jones wanted it. He accepted it, and had the trade-mark ownership transferred to the Tip Corporation. He then developed a lemon-lime drink somewhat similar to 7-Up, and set about selling it to neighboring bottlers. Most of his customers were Pepsi-Cola Bottlers, as were all of his original stockholders. Several of the bottlers sold the lemon-lime type Mountain Dew with a moderate degree of success. Soon it became the leading product manufactured by the Tip Corporation. However, this success was to be short-lived. The Pepsi-Cola Company came out with their lemon-lime drink called Teem, which was backed by an advertising campaign and national coverage. Soon all of the Tip Corporation bottlers of Mountain Dew, abandoned Mountain Dew and took on the Teem franchise which prohibited them from bottling any other lemon-lime drink. Thus, the Tip Corporation fortunes sank to another low ebb.

Mr. Jones was busy, however, in compounding other flavors to offer to bottlers. One of these was a drink similar to Sun Drop, a trade-marked beverage then owned by Char. F. Lazier Co. of St. Louis. Although this drink resembled the lemon-lime drinks somewhat, it contained enough orange juice to remove it from the lemon-lime classifications, and thereby allowed bottlers to produce it even though they had franchises that prohibited the bottling of another lemon-lime drink. After much testing, tasting, and sampling Mr. Jones was ready to offer the drink to the public. He had several names that he tried to choose from, but was still undecided what to call it, when he made a trip through North Carolina to try to find someone to introduce the drink for him. He stopped at Lumberton, North Carolina to see Herman and Charles Minges, two of his fellow stockholders in the Tip Corporation. After testing and tasting and assuring themselves that the taste of the drink was right, the Minges brothers indicated that they would not consider introducing the drink if it required the purchase of special bottles. They said they would bottle and attempt to sell the drink if they could use the old Mountain Dew bottles that they had once used, and that they now had stored in a barn nearby. Herman Minges asked why they could not just call it the New Mountain Dew. As Jones was beginning to become desperate since he had already been turned down by other prospects, he reluctantly agreed.

As for marketing strategy Jones and the Minges' brothers went to a local printer and had some small streamers printed on paper saying, "Try the New Mountain Dew." The salesmen on the trucks were told to try to leave one case at each store they worked. This they did, and on their next trip they were mostly surprised to find that the one case was sold out. The next order was for two cases, and salesmen were cautioned not to over-load any customers, but to let them run out rather than overstock.

In a short time Mountain Dew became the second best selling item for the Minges' brothers at Lumberton, and soon, the word spread to neighboring bottlers. The same sales strategy was followed as these plants were franchised and began selling.

Unfortunately, we are unable to place specific dates on some of the foregoing described actions. However, from the minutes of the stockholders meetings and directors meetings of the Tip Corporation it is known that the date of the original formation of the Tip Corporation of America was July 18th, 1944. The reorganization of the company took place on August 28th, 1957. The first time Mountain Dew is mentioned is in those minutes of the meeting of July 29th, 1959. A report on the sale of New Mountain Dew was given in the meeting of 29th of May 1962. This report was that the New Mountain Dew was showing a great increase in sales.

Now - back to the narrative of Mountain Dew. As stated previously, the news of the success of the New Mountain Dew at Lumberton, North Carolina spread to neighboring bottlers. In a very short time, perhaps a dozen plants in North Carolina and South Carolina started buying, bottling, and selling Mountain Dew. Without exception they found that this new drink soon became their second largest selling drink. Soon requests for Mountain Dew were received from other states, Georgia, Alabama, and Florida. Even several plants in Ohio were also selling Mountain Dew concentrate and were assigned territory. The policy of the Tip Corporation was to first offer the right to sell Mountain Dew to Pepsi-Cola bottlers, but if they did not desire to accept this right, then to offer it to other than Pepsi-Cola bottlers for that territory. Therefore, several bottlers acquired the right to bottle

Mountain Dew who were other than Pepsi-Cola bottlers. Florence, South Carolina, Dr Pepper Bottling Company was one of the first of these bottlers. Another non Pepsi-Cola bottler was Roanoke Dr Pepper Bottling Company. They, too, found Mountain Dew a strong second in sales volume, and in one instance, at least, it became the volume leader.

At any rate by 1964 the Pepsi-Cola Company, whose representatives had watched with amazement the rapid growth in sales of Mountain Dew, approached members of the Board of Directors of the Tip Corporation with the end in view of buying the Tip Corporation. After a bit of haggling an offer was made and accepted in September 1964 to sell the assets of the Tip Corporation to the Pepsi-Cola Company. Since that time the sales of Mountain Dew have grown at a tremendous pace. Given national exposure and promotion by the Pepsi-Cola Company, Mountain Dew has become the seventh largest selling soft drink in the United States by 1980. Sales of Mountain Dew in 1980 exceeded those of many old and widely advertised drinks such as Royal Crown Cola, Orange Crush, Double Cola and others that have been long considered good selling brands.

For the Pepsi-Cola Company, Mountain Dew has become their second best selling drink. It has given them a tool to successfully compete in the so called "flavor" market. This they sorely needed as Pepsi-Cola Bottlers had to look to other sources to find beverages to compete in this market. As a result of the acquisition of Mountain Dew, Pepsi-Cola Company is now able to offer their bottlers strong support in the whole soft drink market.

New bottling plant at 211 Washington Ave. Constructed in 1967 & 1968. Formally opened with much ceremony & fanfare on Sept. 30, 1968. With more than 60,000 square feet of floor space and with new bottling machinery, our capacity to produce 800 bottles of soft drinks per minute.

Chapter X

The years 1965 to 1975 were years of solid achievement and spectacular progress in sales and market dominance by our company. The first portion of the decade was marked by putting into action the earlier dreams we had of acquiring better production and distribution facilities. The latter portion of the decade was marked by the building and perfecting our whole organization to generate and handle the increased business that we were able to do with our new facilities. To illustrate, our total sales in 1965 were just under two million dollars; in 1975, total sales were slightly under eight million dollars. In 1965, 99% of our production was in the 10 oz. package. In 1975, approximately one-half of the production was in the 16 oz. package. So it is evident that many changes took place in this ten year period.

As mentioned in Chapter VIII, it was in the early sixties that we recognized the fact that new and larger facilities were necessary if we were to continue to go forward. It was in the late sixties that we actually acquired some of the most needed of these facilities. A site for a new plant was purchased in 1965 and grading was started on the property. An architect, Mr. Winston Sharpley of Roanoke, was employed and instructed to proceed with the plans. The building was finished in early 1968.

New production machinery was studied, the orders placed, and the machinery was installed in the new plant in 1968. In addition to the new production line, the larger of the two lines we had at the old plant was moved to the new location. As the capacity of the new line was 500 ten ounce bottles per minute and the old line 300 ten ounce bottles per minute making a total of 800 bottles per minute versus a total capacity of 390 bottles per minute at the old plant, it can easily be seen that our capacity to produce bottled beverages was doubled in 1965.

Not only was our production capacity increased, but so was our storage capacity increased several times over. Also, the method of handling was changed from the old lift jack and platform method to the fork lift and pallet system which revolutionized the product handling both here at the plant and in all our warehouses.

It was also in the 1965-1975 decade that we completely changed our delivery fleet to totally enclosed body trucks. Previously, we had used the cheaper open type bodies which gave little or no protection to our products from the weather or dusty or dirty conditions. Therefore our plans to better protect our products until they reached the consumer were given a big assist.

Changes in methods of product handling and increased business brought on needs for additional warehouse facilities. So during the decade under review we built new, added to, remodeled and updated all of our warehouse facilities. In the Hillsville - Galax area we built a new warehouse on a new location and combined two warehouses. At Lebanon, we built a new warehouse on a new location. At Bristol and Pulaski, we added space by constructing additions to the buildings that existed. All warehouses were equipped with loading docks and lift trucks to conform with our new materials handling equipment.

Between 1965 and 1975, a revolution took place in package sizes and containers used in the bottling industry and in our case this was particularly true. For the previous sixty years of the bottled beverage history of this locality, the only package had been the glass returnable bottle. The size of the bottle had changed, but the returnable glass bottle was the only package that was used to any extent in the industry. Now in a very brief period of time we found a large market for other packages. For instance: our sales of the conventional package of 10 oz. to 16 oz. glass returnable bottles actually dropped from 1,448,333 cases in 1965 to 1,253,341 cases in 1975. However,

Office force, Plant personnel and Sales force at the time of the formal opening of the new plant in 1968.

during that time 12 oz. cans became a factor in the market and our sales of cans increased from 8,834 cases in 1965 to 681,340 cases in 1975. Also, we sold no quarts in 1965, while in 1975 we sold 96,664 cases. Sales of premix and syrup for use in fountains showed increases of approximately the same proportions.

The net results of these package changes and container changes was that during this period the actual amount of soft drinks in volume, whether measured by ounces or gallons, practically doubled. This increase in volume coupled with several increases of prices during this period enabled us to show a dollar volume of nearly four times from the years of 1965 to 1975.

Another milestone of our progress was the acquisition of the Dr Pepper Franchise in 1971. It was in that year that we bought the assets of the Dr Pepper Bottling Company of Marion and thereby secured the franchise to bottle Dr Pepper, and also because that company also bottled Seven Up, we acquired the Seven Up Franchise for that portion of our territory that the Dr Pepper Bottling Company had.

The Dr Pepper Bottling Company of Marion was established in Marion in the late 1930's by a Mr. Vanhoy of either West Jefferson or North Wilkesboro, North Carolina in the building on Main Street now occupied by Model Beauty Salon. Mr. Vanhoy operated the business for a very short period of time and sold it to Mr. Forester and Mr. Clay Church of North Wilkesboro. Mr. Church moved to Marion and operated the business for several years. When Mr. Church was drafted in the World War II, the business was managed by Mr. Marvin Groseclose until Mr. Church returned in 1947. It was shortly after Mr. Church resumed operation of the business that he had personal financial troubles and the business was taken over by Mr. Forester. Mr. Forester was a prominent businessman of West Jefferson and he operated the Dr Pepper business with a series of managers. Mr. Groseclose ran the business very successfully for several years until he died. He was succeeded by Mr. Phillips, who likewise died in a short time. In the meantime, Mr. Forester died, and the business was then operated by the Northwestern Bank of North Wilkesboro, administrator of the Estate of Mr. Forester, who sent Mr. Robert Church, son of Mr. Clay Church to Marion to run the business. The results of this operation were not acceptable to the bank and the decision to sell was made after we made them an offer to buy.

The purchase of the Dr Pepper Bottling Company proved to be a very valuable asset for Marion Bottling Company. It gave us some added volume, and at the same time eliminated a very troublesome competitor. We were able to increase the volume of both Dr Pepper and Seven Up as we could give these two fine soft drinks so much better exposure to the public through our vending machines which greatly outnumbered those available to them previously. At the same time, the costs for production and distribution were much less for the combination than by separate and duplicating organizations.

Another development in this period was our participation in and the development of a corporation that was named Appalachian Packaging Corporation. As noted before in this recital, we found ourselves caught up in a packaging revolution in the bottling industry during the period of time under review. One of the most outstanding changes was the preference the public showed to purchasing their favorite drinks from cans. Canning was an entirely different operation from bottling, as different machinery and equipment is required to can beverages. We started by buying our canned beverages from a canning plant in Lynchburg and later switched to a plant in Princeton, West, Va. Our volume in this package increased to the point that it became a sizable part of our business, and we realized that we should be making the full profit ourselves instead of sharing it with others.

Left to Right:
TOM STORER - Regional Manager, Pepsi-Cola
W. M. HULL, JR. - Board Chairman, Marion Bottling Company
PRESTON S. COPENHAVER - President, Marion Bottling Company
DON TURNBULL - District Manager, Pepsi-Cola
1972 - Award of placque for exceeding 200 bottles of Pepsi-Cola per capita.

However, when we investigated we found that we had no where near the volume necessary to operate a canning plant profitably.

Therefore, after finding several other bottlers in the same situation, we engaged ourselves in helping organize a corporation to build and operate a canning plant on a co-op basis. In other words, the corporation would can the canned beverages needed by the member bottlers and would be operated with the intention of selling to the members their requirements of canned beverages at cost or near cost to the co-op.

Such a corporation was started in 1970 and completed in 1971 and was named Appalachian Packaging Corporation with plant and offices at Knoxville, Tenn. We became owner of 13.9% of the stock and Preston S. Copenhaver, Jr. was elected Secretary-Treasurer and a member of the executive committee. Our investment of $27,800.00 for our 13.9% interest in the corporation was a very fine investment and was repaid many times over in the succeeding years in the low price we were able to obtain on our supply of canned soft drinks. Canned soft drinks continue to increase in sales volume.

It was in 1968 that the most publicized event in the history of Marion Bottling Company took place. That was the opening and formal dedication of the new plant at the new location at 211 Washington Avenue. After weeks of planning and scheduling and with assistance from the Pepsi-Cola Company the formal plant opening was held on September 28th, 1968. We had as special guest of honor Joan Crawford who at that time was a member of the Board of Directors of Pepsi-Cola Company and James Sommerall, President of Pepsi-Cola Company. We had advance publicity and news coverage of all the proceedings, which included a dinner at Martha Washington Inn in Abingdon for several hundred of our largest customers, local officials, including our Congressman, Mr. William Wampler and other prominent people. Pictures of the guests of honor and of the proceedings were published in the local papers as well as regional papers such as The Roanoke Times and The Bristol Herald Courier. Out-of-town guests included bottler friends from many parts of the country. A write-up of the events in the trade journals of the industry gave us favorable publicity on a nationwide coverage.

One of the more important things that the 1965-1975 period produced was the betterment of our employees' various benefit plans. Our group insurance plan was vastly expanded to keep the benefits in step with the rapidly increasing cost of medical attention. Also, our vacation plan was liberalized and paid vacations lengthened. It was in this same period that the fully trusted pension plan was established. This plan funded solely by contribution of the company, combined with Social Security payments, enabled the employees of Marion Bottling Company to retire at the normal retirement age without having to severely change their standard of living. These things, coupled with the numerous wage increases that were given during this time produced a group of loyal employees that supported the company all the way in its successful attempt to be, and stay, the leader of the soft drink manufacturer in the area.

The period of time under review also produced the greatest organizational change since 1929. Since that time, the chief operating officer of the company had been the writer. In 1929, he was Secretary-Treasurer and Manager of the company. At a later date, he became President and Treasurer and as such the Chief Operating Officer and retained this position until 1970 when the office of President and Chief Operating Officer was handed to Preston S. Copenhaver, Jr. Wythe M. Hull, Jr. became Chairman of the Board at this time. I. Hugh Slagle was made Treasurer of the company after having served as Assistant Treasurer for several years. This team of officers proved to be the very thing that was needed to push forward to the best years of the company.

Chapter XI

This, the last chapter of this recital of the past of Marion Bottling Company, Inc., deals with the most exciting and dynamic years of the company. It also records the years of the greatest prosperity of the company, of plans for the future and the sudden switch of fortunes occassioned by the illness and death of the Chief Operating Officer, Preston S. Copenhaver, Jr. The years covered are from 1975 through April 1983.

In the previous chapter, we recited that the demand by the public for more sizes of packages in their favorite soft drinks had caused us to build a new plant and equip it with new machinery of greater capacity to meet the needs of the market place. This trend continued far beyond our expectations, and coupled with the addition of a number of new versions of the trade-marked drinks, (Pepsi-Cola, Diet Pepsi-Cola, Pepsi Free, etc.) all in several sized packages, soon made our manufacturing improvements of 1968 obsolete and we needed more space for production and storage and additional machinery and equipment. Our acquisition of the Dr Pepper Bottling Co. in 1971 proved to be a very wise investment in many ways and really began to prove it's worth in the time period we have under consideration. With these things in mind, we planned and executed the plan to enlarge and expand our new plant building. Also, included was the addition of a new and separate building to house the vending operation.

The architect who designed and planned the 1968 building had retired from the business, so we selected the architectural firm of Smithey & Boynton, Inc. of Roanoke to be the architects for our expansion. After much research and study, the plans were completed and the project advertised for bids. The low bidder on the job was James R. VanHoy & Sons, Inc. of West Jefferson, N.C. Construction was started in 1979 and completed in 1981. The low bid for the building project was $1,406,425.00. Besides providing for additional manufacturing and storage space for manufactured products, provisions were made for much needed additional office space for the executive offices as well as office space for sales and marketing personnel. Additional space was provided for a new laboratory and testing room. The cafeteria and dining area was remodeled as was the office area that was to house a new computer with its satellite stations. And, as was stated previously, a complete new building was added for storage, service and display of vending equipment. This building, a two-story building complete with elevator, is proving to be a great assist in the rapidly growing and very important vending segment of the business.

During the 1975-83 era, the prolification of new packages, both in design and size continued far beyond our planning of the nineteen sixties. Plastic bottles replaced glass bottles in the large sizes and non-returnable glass bottles began to appear on the market place. Our machinery, which we so proudly claimed to be modern and up-to-date in the sixties, became obsolete in the seventies. Therefore, in order to maintain our leadership in the market, we decided to re-equip our bottling line in 1977 and 1978. We purchased more than $1,000,000.00 of bottling line equipment in these two years and thereby increased our capacity for production by approximately 100% in the conventional sized packages; but also acquired the ability to produce beverages in plastic bottles, with screw cap closures and regular closures to produce regular glass packages with either screw cap or regular crown closures; to either wash bottles in the regular and time tested manner or to rinse only the new bottles, plastic or glass; to package the bottle in wooden, plastic or cardboard cases. We also added a depalletizer to our already functioning palletizer outlay of machinery and thereby eliminate at least one manual handling of the bottles. Also added was a completely covered bottling conveyor from the washer or rinser to the filler. The new filler was installed at this time had a rated capacity of 1,000 bottles per minute on the 10 oz. size. We were never able to get performance at this rate, but it did do more than its rated capacity at the larger size bottle projected speeds and it did greatly increase our production capacity of all sized products.

The last large addition to our production equipment and machinery was made in 1982 when a complete new water treatment plant was installed. This replaced the water treatment plant we had been using since 1967 and it more than doubled the amount of completely treated and purified water we were able to produce.

All these additions and replacements of machinery contributed to our ability to produce high quality products at the lowest possible cost and thereby enabled us to always be able to meet competition on a favorable price basis. This fact enabled us to help maintain a favorable market because our competition was aware of our capabilities and they were very cautious about starting any wild price wars that were commonplace in surrounding markets.

During our building and equipment expansion, we did not neglect our office space, which up to this time had been barely adequate. During the building program of 1967-68, we cut back on office space and quality to a very minimum as we attempted to hold our building to the planned budget. At that time, much of the funds for the building were borrowed funds and therefore we were very cautious; now however, we started our program with funds in hand to complete the project. We needed more office space and we also felt we could afford nicer equipped offices for our executive personnel. We also needed space specifically adapted to computers which we found could be of much value to our operations. Therefore, we added four new executive offices, a large specially designed computer room, a remodelled and redecorated employee's cafeteria and dining room and a series of smaller offices for our sales supervisors. The estimated costs for refurnishing the offices and for the new office equipment required amounted to $146,554.00.

The period under review continued to be one in which the vending part of our business became increasingly important. The phase out of the small grocery stores and the family operated small filling stations and stores made vending a very important part of the business. The new vending building previously described was one step in our intention of becoming the leader in the vending of soft drinks in our area, but in addition to better facilities for servicing the machines, many more vending machines of better quality and of course at a higher cost per machine were required. In the period of 1976-1982 our company purchased and put into use vending machines that cost a total of $3,135,190.00. By continually increasing the number of vending machines on location and by continuing to work at securing better locations for our vending machines, we were able to more than compensate for the continual shrinking of the number of small grocery stores of the Mom & Pop variety that seem to be victims of the economy.

During all these improvements and additions to our manufacturing plant in the years 1975-1983, we did not neglect our automotive fleet. It was in 1975, that we placed the order for the largest number of route trucks in the history of the company. Also during the period of time under consideration, we began buying larger route trucks to be able to handle our expanded variety of packages. We bought 10 or 12 Bay trucks instead of 8 Bay trucks. We also began buying diesel engines in our route trucks which we found to be more economical to operate than those powered with gasoline engines. Also added to our fleet were several special purpose trucks such as the panel body trucks used for sampling as a means of advertising.

The one big thing that was different about this major expansion of the facilities of the business and other major expansions of the past was that this time we were able to pay for all phases of the expansion with funds that were generated by the business itself. No borrowing of money was necessary and we were able to continue to pay dividends, and in fact, increase the amount of dividends to our stockholders at the same time. Also, we continually raised wages during the period to keep pace or exceed the rate of inflation that was taking place. Our prices, naturally, were increased several times but were always competitive and in most instances the prices of our products were below the prices being paid for the same brands in most of our adjoining territory. At all times, wages paid our employees compared most favorably with the wages being paid to our competitors employees, as well as being well in line with wages paid by local employers in other industries.

In recent years it has become increasingly hard to find any yardstick or other measuring device to compare results of the business done at different times. At one time, we judged our progress mainly by the number of cases of our product produced. This method has become obsolete because of the multiple packages, sizes, etc. Now we sell much more of our products in cans or in pre-mix machines or in syrup machines than formerly. Therefore, we now find the best comparison to be in dollars of sales. That of course must be adjusted due to inflation as the value of the dollar continues to decrease. However this may be, the fact remains that the expansion program just reviewed reacted very favorably to our business. From 1975 to 1982 our sales increased dollarwise 370%. Our profits increased likewise with the percentage figures being 239%. These figures were started from a most satisfactory base in 1975, so the evidence is that the reinvestment of quite a sum of money in the business was a success.

During the foregoing recital of the happenings at Marion Bottling Company, Inc. for the preceeding half century, very little has been said about the most valuable asset the company managed to acquire in that time. That asset was the dedicated, competent and loyal group of people who were the employees of the company. Deliberate effort has been made to avoid mentioning names as so many have contributed so much that it would be impossible to give proper recognition to all these people without leaving out many of the most deserving ones. From a payroll of only five persons in 1929, the payroll continued to grow to 179 persons in 1983. This group of people in 1983 contained 19 persons who had been employees of the company for more than 25 years.

It was from these people that most of the innovative ideas of the operation of the company came from. All through the years, they were consulted and it was from their ideas and suggestions that management established policies, rules and procedures that in later years gave us the reputation, locally, statewide, and, yes, nationally to some extent, of being one of the best run Pepsi-Cola Bottling plants in the whole country.

From the very beginning of the company, we tried to train our people to do the best job possible. Very early, we established the custom of holding sales meetings to better train our sales people. At first we did not have much help from the franchise drink companies with material and information, but later on a great deal of help was obtained from them along this line. We took every opportunity to train our production people by having them attend meetings, schools, etc. that were provided by the franchise companies from time to time and as we could afford it, we had some of our personnel attend the annual bottlers conventions to bring back all of the new ideas they could garner from that source. Our garage mechanics and personnel were encouraged to attend all available instructive sessions put on by the motor companies. By careful selection of new employees and by continual training and encouraging old employees we did assemble a group of people who were really experts in their lines. By trying to treat these people

Aerial view of new construction and remodeling (in progess) of the plant made in 1980 & 1981. The foundations for the new Vender Service building can be seen in the extreme left side of the photo.

fairly and equally, we received in return loyalty and trust and an input of ideas that was the greatest single ingredient in our success as a growing operation. On three different occasions, attempts were made to unionize our group. It would have been a prize indeed for any union that could have succeded in claiming Marion Bottling Company as a member of their union. On all these attempts, our people remained loyal and the union attempts were soundly defeated each time.

Not only have our employees been loyal and dedicated to their employer, they have likewise been good citizens and as such have supported schools, churches and community enterprises in a most creditable manner. The payroll of the company, amounting in 1982 to more than $2,800,000.00 has almost all been spent in the communities where the employees live. Needless to say, this annual payroll supported many others than just those to whom the paycheck was written. Stores, shops, service people of all descriptions, shared in the prosperity of the company and its employees.

The splendid relationship that existed between the employees and the company was encouraged and fostered by several things the company did for their employees as a continuing policy. After we were able to break the necessary economic restraints forced on us by the stubborn refusal of the industry to break the five cent selling price of soft drinks and thus place a ceiling on the wholesale price, we hastened to adjust upward our wages and other employee benefits. We were, I believe, the first bottler in the area to give a hospital insurance plan to our employees. This plan was updated and increased in benefits from time to time. We were the first bottler in the area to give all employees paid vacations. This plan, too, was upgraded several times. We added to and continued with our plan of paid holidays, although at first competition tried to use this to their advantage by not observing the holidays. Wages were increased many times to bring into line our wages with not only what other bottling companies were paying their employees but also in line with what other industries in the area were paying their employees.

A pension plan was established, that was funded solely by the company. This was a Trusteed Plan that the company placed funds in trust with the First National Exchange Bank of Roanoke that were determined to be sufficient to pay to each employee, a pension after retirement, which combined with Social Security would equal three-fourths of the employees rate of pay at retirement.

A bonus plan that paid each employee a bonus at Christmas time was also established and in force for forty-five years. This plan continued to increase in the amount paid out to employees until by 1982 the total of Christmas bonuses amounted to $111,345.00. The plan was designed to give increased recognition to those employees who had the greater seniority in service with the company.

And so it was this splendid relationship between employer and employee that brought about the excellent group of people that made up the personnel of Marion Bottling Company.

So far in this chapter, we have recorded the very fine condition of the Marion Bottling Company was in at the period of time between 1975 and 1983. From the standpoint of sales, profits, physical equipment, organization and personnel, the appraisal had to be classified as excellent. Outlook for the future did indeed seem bright. It must be recorded, however, that often unseen or unanticipated events change plans drastically. This was the case of Marion Bottling Company. In October, 1981, Preston S. Copenhaver, Jr., President and Chief Operating Officer first noticed that he tired easily and later developed a cough that sent him seeking medical advice. It was determined that he had cancer in one lung. Immediately he began taking treatments and for nearly a year, the reports were optimistic. He thought, as did his doctors, that the condition was under control and he had hopes for a complete remission. That was not to be, however, and in November, 1982, he was told that the malady was spreading and out of control.

During his year of treatments, the writer attempted to attend to the duties of the office of President as well as his own as Chairman of the Board. However, when it became apparent that Mr. Copenhaver would never be able to resume his duties, a conference was held and it was decided that the fact that no replacement for Mr. Copenhaver was in sight and due to the fact that the office required a strong and knowledgeable person, the best solution would be to sell the company to someone who could provide that kind of person, if it was possible to get a satisfactory price for all our stockholders. Consequently, a number of potential buyers were contacted immediately and notified that the company could be purchased under certain limitations such as employment contracts for key personnel; the purchase of 100% of the stock or at least an offer to purchase 100% at the offered price; an all cash, no stock deal and a retention of the right to accept or refuse any offer made without having to account for such activities. The response to this action was amazing. At least eight definite offers to purchase were eventually received and many more were interested but withdrew when they sensed that the purchase price would be beyond their ability to finance.

In early January, Mr. Copenhaver was taken back to the Baptist Hospital at Winston-Salem and he died there on January 11, 1983. Naturally, all negotations for the sale of the plant were suspended for a short period of time, but were resumed about the first of February. The list of prospective buyers was finally reduced to two, Atlantic Pepsi-Cola Company and R.K.O. Pepsi-Cola Bottlers, both companies wholly owned subsidiaries of large conglomerates with many diversified interests. We finally decided to sell to R.K.O. Pepsi-Cola Bottlers, largely because of what we perceived to be a better record of retaining the personnel of the plants they acquired; both prospective purchasers having offered substantially the same amount of money for the deal. A contract to sell and a contract to buy was executed by Marion Bottling Company and R.K.O. Bottlers while the final details and plans for transfer were drawn up.

This story would not be complete or appropriate without paying tribute to the splendid record of performance of Preston S. Copenhaver, Jr. in bringing the peak of perfection in his tenure of office from 1970 to 1983 as Chief Operating Officer of the company. It was he who was the moving spirit of the last large expansion of the physical assets of Marion Bottling Company and who had plans for future expansions. His abilities as a leader were recognized by his comtemporaries as shown by his election to the Board of Directors of the Pepsi-Cola Bottlers Association and to several of it's important committies. His fellow bottlers elected him President of the Virginia Soft Drink Association and made him Chairman of it's important P.A.C. Committee.

And so the story ends with the final transfer of capital stock in the corporation from Marion Bottling Company, Inc. to R.K.O. Bottlers, Inc. on April 29, 1983. The production of fine soft drinks will continue to grow and the business will continue to furnish good employment to good people but this time from outside direction and supervision. There will be many changes in methods of operation, many for the betterment of the people who work for the company, but there will be new adjustments to be made. We wish for the new owners another three-quarters of a century of growth and prosperity.